T0413165

Too Cute!
Baby Horses

by Betsy Rathburn

BELLWETHER MEDIA
MINNEAPOLIS, MN

BLASTOFF!
Beginners

Blastoff! Beginners are developed by literacy experts and educators to meet the needs of early readers. These engaging informational texts support young children as they begin reading about their world. Through simple language and high frequency words paired with crisp, colorful photos, Blastoff! Beginners launch young readers into the universe of independent reading.

Blastoff! Universe

Reading Level — Grade K

Grades 1-3

Grade 4

Sight Words in This Book 🔍

and	get	run	with
at	good	the	
away	in	they	
can	look	this	
eat	on	to	
find	play	up	

This edition first published in 2022 by Bellwether Media, Inc.

No part of this publication may be reproduced in whole or in part without written permission of the publisher. For information regarding permission, write to Bellwether Media, Inc., Attention: Permissions Department, 6012 Blue Circle Drive, Minnetonka, MN 55343.

Library of Congress Cataloging-in-Publication Data

Names: Rathburn, Betsy, author.
Title: Baby horses / by Betsy Rathburn.
Description: Minneapolis, MN : Bellwether Media, 2022. | Series: Blastoff! beginners: Too cute! | Includes bibliographical references and index. | Audience: Ages 4-7 | Audience: Grades K-1
Identifiers: LCCN 2021001465 (print) | LCCN 2021001466 (ebook) | ISBN 9781644874875 (library binding) | ISBN 9781648344695 (paperback) | ISBN 9781648343957 (ebook)
Subjects: LCSH: Foals--Juvenile literature.
Classification: LCC SF285.3 .R38 2022 (print) | LCC SF285.3 (ebook) | DDC 636.1--dc23
LC record available at https://lccn.loc.gov/2021001465
LC ebook record available at https://lccn.loc.gov/2021001466

Editor: Amy McDonald   Designer: Jeffrey Kollock

Printed in the United States of America, North Mankato, MN.

Table of Contents

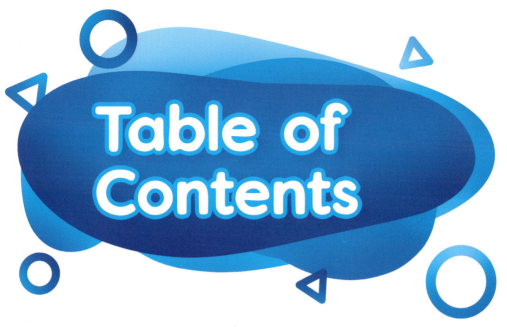

A Baby Horse!

Look at the
baby horse.
Hello, foal!

Farm Life

Foals live
on farms.
They stay
close to mom.

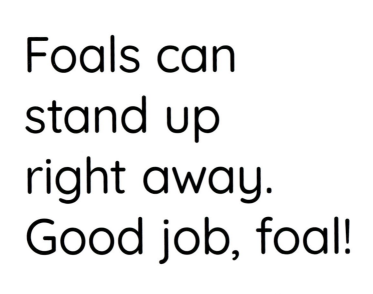

Foals can
stand up
right away.
Good job, foal!

Foals sleep in **stables**. They stay warm in soft bedding.

stable

bedding

Foals **nurse**.
They drink
mom's milk.

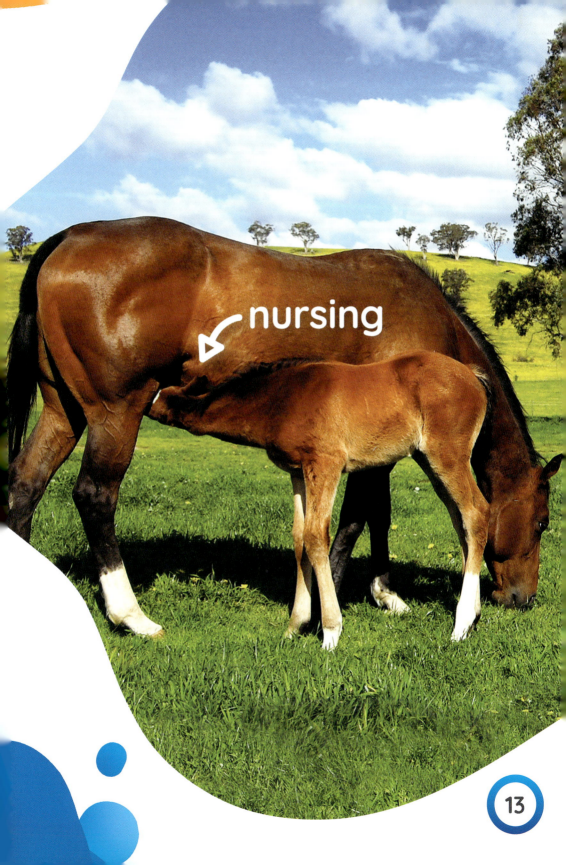

nursing

Foals eat hay.
They find grass
in **pastures**.

pasture

hay

Foals play
with friends.
They run
and **buck**!

bucking

Growing Up

Foals get
stronger.
They grow
taller.

This foal
runs fast.
Goodbye, mom!

Baby Horse Facts

Horse Life Stages

foal   yearling   adult

A Day in the Life

eat grass   run in   spend time
             pastures   with mom

Glossary

buck

to jump into
the air and kick
up back legs

nurse

to drink
mom's milk

pastures

open places
where animals
eat grass

stables

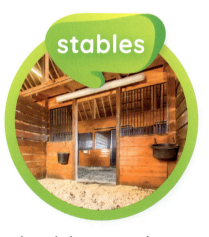

buildings where
horses live

To Learn More

ON THE WEB

FACTSURFER

Factsurfer.com gives you
a safe, fun way to find
more information.

1. Go to www.factsurfer.com.

2. Enter "baby horses" into the search box
and click 🔍.

3. Select your book cover to see a list
of related content.

Index

The images in this book are reproduced through the courtesy of: Eric Isselee, front cover, pp. 4, 5, 8, 22 (foal, adult); mariait, p. 3; DragoNika, pp. 6-7; Lillac, pp. 8-9; Artazum, p. 10; Alla-Berlezova, pp. 10-11; Maria Junge Fotografie, pp. 12-13; Irina Mos, pp. 14, 23 (pastures); Victoria Rak, pp. 14-15; imageBROKER/ Alamy, pp. 16-17; Makarova Viktoria, p. 18; Binja Schmidt, pp. 18-19; Jitka Cernohorska, pp. 20-21; MediaWorldImages/ Alamy, p. 22 (yearling); Lars Christensen, p. 22 (eat); Kwadrat, p. 22 (run); Soloveva Kseniia, p. 22 (mom); el-ka, p. 23 (buck); Iuliia Khabibullina, p. 23 (nurse); Chen's Photos, p. 23 (stables).